T5-CCK-361

6 WORLD PERCUSSION AFRO-CUBAN

Student Edition
By José Antonio Diaz

Related MP3 Files
for Home Practice Accessible at
www.music-expressions.com

Music Expressions™

Expressions Music Curriculum™, Music Expressions™, Band Expressions™, Jazz Expressions™,
Orchestra Expressions™, Choral Expressions™, Piano Expressions™, and Guitar Expressions™
are trademarks of Warner Bros. Publications. All Rights Reserved.

1 2 3 4 5 6 7 8 9 10   09 08 07 06 05 04

Warner Bros. Publications • 15800 NW 48th Avenue • Miami, FL 33014

GENERAL MUSIC
COMPLETE TEACHER EDITION (EMC6001)
UPC: 6-54979-07099-3
ISBN: 0-7579-1849-2 90000

TEACHER EDITION, VOLUME I (EMC6001A)
UPC: 6-54979-07332-1
ISBN: 0-7579-1949-9 90000

TEACHER EDITION, VOLUME II (EMC6001B)
UPC: 6-54979-07335-2
ISBN: 0-7579-1951-0 90000

TEACHER EDITION, VOLUME III (EMC6001C)
UPC: 6-54979-07336-9
ISBN: 0-7579-1952-9 90000

STUDENT EDITION (EMC6002)
UPC: 6-54979-07221-8
ISBN: 0-7579-1908-1 90000

ORFF ENSEMBLE MODULE (EMC6010)
UPC: 6-54979-08158-6
ISBN: 0-7579-2337-2 90000

AFRO-CUBAN PERCUSSION MODULE
TEACHER EDITION (EMC6009CD)
UPC: 6-54979-07955-2
ISBN: 0-7579-2270-8 90000

STUDENT EDITION (EMC6009S)
UPC: 6-54979-07956-9
ISBN: 0-7579-2271-6 90000

MIDI KEYBOARD MODULE
TEACHER EDITION (EMC6011CD)
UPC: 6-54979-08260-6
ISBN: 0-7579-2383-6 90000

STUDENT EDITION (EMC6011S)
UPC: 6-54979-08261-3
ISBN: 0-7579-2384-4 90000

MUSICAL MODULE: IT'S ALL ABOUT MUSIC!
TEACHER EDITION (EMC6012CD)
UPC: 6-54979-08259-0
ISBN: 0-7579-2382-8 90000

STUDENT EDITION (EMC6012S)
UPC: 6-54979-08263-7
ISBN: 0-7579-2387-9 90000

Credits

PROJECT CREATORS & COORDINATORS

Robert W. Smith

Susan L. Smith

AUTHOR

José Antonio Diaz
Houston, Texas

LESSONS CONTENT EDITOR

Linda T. Lovins, Ph.D.
Tallahassee, Florida

MUSIC EXPRESSIONS AUTHORS GRADES 6–8

Timothy S. Brophy, Ph.D.
General Music
Author/Assessment Specialist
University of Florida
Gainesville, Florida

Randy DeLelles
Jeff Kriske
Orff Ensemble Authors
Las Vegas, Nevada

José Antonio Diaz
General Music/World
Percussion Author
Houston, Texas

Michael Gallina, Ed.D.
Jill Gallina
Musicals Authors
Millington, New Jersey

Margaret Griffin
Songwriting Author
Hillsborough County
Public Schools
Tampa, Florida

Darla S. Hanley, Ph.D.
General Music/Music in the
Media Author
Musical Lessons Consultant
Shenandoah University
Winchester, Virginia

June M. Hinckley
General Music/
Songwriting Author
Midi Keyboard and Orff
Ensemble Lessons Consultant
Department of Education
Tallahassee, Florida

Janice Lancaster
Songwriting Author
Hillsborough County
Public Schools
Tampa, Florida

Carolyn C. Minear
General Music Author
Orange County Public Schools
Orlando, Florida

Don Muro
Music Technology Author
St. James, New York

ORCHESTRA

Michael L. Alexander
Houston, Texas

Gerald E. Anderson
Los Angeles, California

Kathleen DeBerry
Brungard
Charlotte, North Carolina

Sandra Dackow
Trenton, New Jersey

Anne C. Witt
Arlington, Texas

BAND

James Campbell
Lexington, Kentucky

Richard C. Crain
The Woodland, Texas

Linda Gammon
Fairfax, Virginia

Gary Markham
Atlanta, Georgia

Michael Story
Houston, Texas

JAZZ

Peter BarenBregge
Upper Marlboro, Maryland

José Antonio Diaz
Houston, Texas

J. Richard Dunscomb
Atlanta, Georgia

Dr. Willie L. Hill, Jr.
Amherst, Massachusetts

Jerry Tolson
Louisville, Kentucky

CHORAL

Amy Alibon
Haltorn, Texas

Jim Kimmell
Nashville, Tennessee

Josephine Lee
Chicago, Illinois

Stan McGill
Garland, Texas

Dr. Russell L. Robinson
Gainesville, Florida

GUITAR

Aaron Stang
Miami, Florida

Bill Purse
Pittsburgh, Pennsylvania

RECORDING

Robert Dingley
Executive Producer

Robert W. Smith
Producer

Jack Lamb
Associate Producer

Kendall Thomsen
Recording and Mix Engineer

Andy De Ganahl
Mix Engineer

Jason May
Assistant Mix Engineer

Linda Nelson
Recording Assistance

WARNER BROS. PUBLICATIONS

Fred Anton
CEO

Robert Dingley
Vice President: Education

David Hakim
Vice President: Sales

Andrea Nelson
Vice President: Marketing

Lourdes Carreras-Balepogi
Marketing Coordinator

David Olsen
Director: Business Affairs

PRODUCTION

Gayle Giese
Project Manager/Editor

Heather Mahone
Production Editor

Nadine DeMarco
Editorial Assistant/
Text Proofreader

Donna Wheeler
Editorial Assistance

Nancy Rehm
Senior Art Director

Carmen Fortunato
Art Layout

Martha Ramirez
Spanish Translations and
Phonetic Pronunciations/
Student Book Art Coordination

Ken Rehm
Cover Design

Judit Martinez
Art Layout: Peripheral Pages

Al Nigro
Music Engraving Manager

Glenda Mikell
Music Engraver

Glyn Dryhurst
Director, Production Services

Hank Fields
Production Control Manager

Sharon Marlow
Production Control
Assistant Manager

ACKNOWLEDGMENTS
Special thanks to:

Gino Silva, Art Director, Scholastic Marketing Partners, Scholastic Inc., for logo design.

Remo, Inc., LP Latin Percussion, and West Music for instrument photos.

Ed Uribe, author of *The Essence of Afro-Cuban Percussion & Drum Set* and *The Essence of Brazilian Percussion & Drum Set,* for the use of his photographs.

Credits

Mary Ezquerro-Garcia and Martin Cohen (LP product photos) for the photo of the cha-cha bell on page 14.

Mike Finkelstein, Aaron Stang, and Ray Brych for their help securing photos.

ILLUSTRATION CREDITS
(Student Edition page/Teacher Edition page)

2–3/4. **Lisa Greene Mane**

4–5/6. **Olivia Novak**

6–7/11–12. **Ken Rehm**

8–9/13–14. **Candy Woolley**

10–11/15. **Robert Ramsay**

12–13/21. **Judit Martinez**

14–15/22, 24. **Janel Harrison**

16–17/25. **Nancy Rehm**

18–19/25. **Jorge Paredes**

20–21/26. **Nancy Rehm**

22–23/31. **Ernesto Ebanks**

24–33/36–45. **Lisa Greene Mane**

34–35/40. **Ken Rehm**

36–37/51. **Judit Martinez**

38–39/52. **Jorge Paredes**

40–41/52. **Robert Ramsay**

42–47/57–61. **Candy Woolley**

48–49/65. **Martha Ramirez**

50–51/66. **Olivia Novak**

52–53/67–68. **Thais Yanes**

54–55/73. **Candy Woolley**

56–57/74. **Ken Rehm**

58–59/85–86. **Janel Harrison**

60–65/90–95. **Robert Ramsay**

66–69/96–98. **Joe Klucar**

70–71/110–111. **Ernesto Ebanks**

72–73/112–113. **Olivia Novak**

74–75/114–115. **Judit Martinez**

PHOTO CREDITS
(Student Edition page/Teacher Edition page)

4–5/6. **Musical Instruments: © Corbis Musical Instruments**

8–9/13–14. **Cha-cha bell: Photo courtesy of Mary Ezquerro-Garcia, Martin Cohen (LP product photos)**

12–13/12–13. **Tito Puente: © Corbis**

22–23/31. **© Hulton-Deutsch Collection/Corbis**

48–49/65. **Celia Cruz: © Manuel Zambrana/Corbis**

50–51/66. **Piano: Corbis Musical Instruments**

Contents

THE ROOTS OF AFRO~CUBAN MUSIC

MEXICO

CUBA

BRAZIL

ARGENTINA

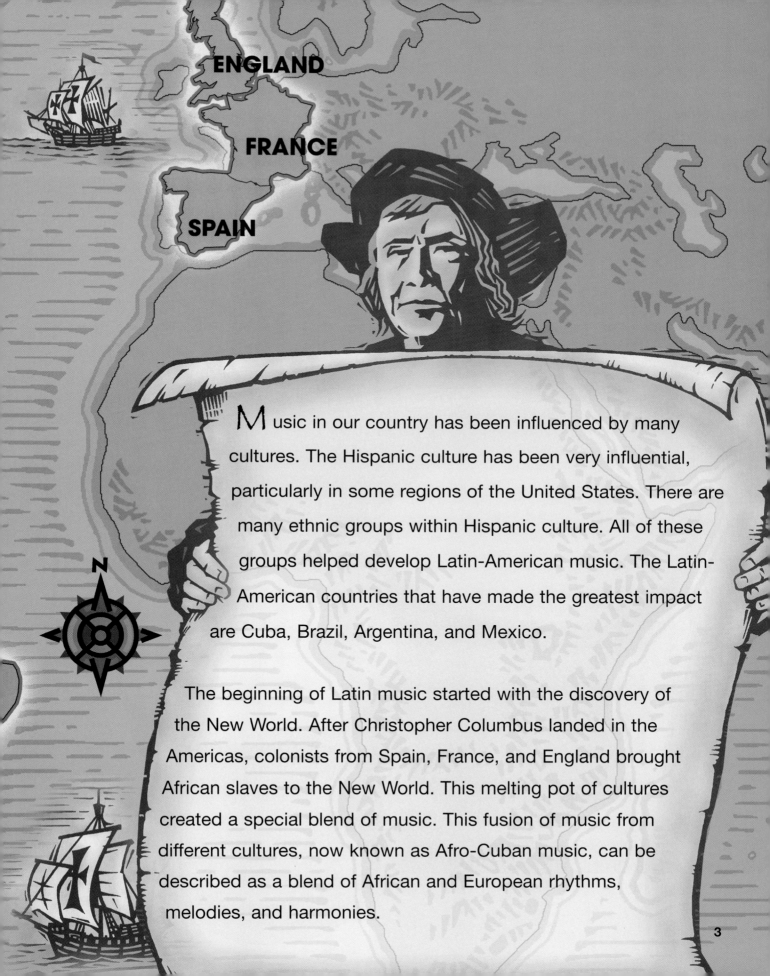

ENGLAND

FRANCE

SPAIN

N

Music in our country has been influenced by many cultures. The Hispanic culture has been very influential, particularly in some regions of the United States. There are many ethnic groups within Hispanic culture. All of these groups helped develop Latin-American music. The Latin-American countries that have made the greatest impact are Cuba, Brazil, Argentina, and Mexico.

The beginning of Latin music started with the discovery of the New World. After Christopher Columbus landed in the Americas, colonists from Spain, France, and England brought African slaves to the New World. This melting pot of cultures created a special blend of music. This fusion of music from different cultures, now known as Afro-Cuban music, can be described as a blend of African and European rhythms, melodies, and harmonies.

3-2 Son Clave

JOSÉ ANTONIO DIAZ

Play four times.

I can play this beat. I can play this beat.

2-3 Son Clave

JOSÉ ANTONIO DIAZ

This beat   I   can   play.   This beat   I   can   play.

5

CHA-CHA

The **cha-cha,** originally known as the cha-cha-cha, is one of the most popular Afro-Cuban musical forms. This medium-slow dance rhythm became popular during the 1950s. The first cha-cha composition, titled "La Engañadora," was written in 1951 by Cuban violinist Enrique Jorrin. This dance style received its name from the scraping sounds of dancers' feet.

"Oye Cómo Va," meaning "Listen to How It Goes," is one of the best-known cha-cha compositions. Tito Puente, a legendary percussionist, wrote "Oye Cómo Va." Pop star Carlos Santana's arrangement of this cha-cha classic became a huge hit in 1971.

OYE CÓMO VA

Words and Music by
TITO PUENTE
Arranged by VICTOR LOPEZ

O-ye có-mo va,   mi rit - mo,   bue-no pa' go-zar,   mu -la - ta.

Claves

Claves are percussion instruments traditionally made of two pieces of wood. These two wooden pieces, when struck together, produce a high-pitched sound. The claves are used to perform a specific pattern as a guideline for various Afro-Cuban rhythms.

JOSÉ ANTONIO DIAZ

Example A

Claves

This beat   I   can   play.   This beat   I   can   play.

JOSÉ ANTONIO DIAZ

Example B

Cha-cha Bell

Cha-Cha Bell

The cha-cha bell is a small high-pitched bell that is used extensively in the cha-cha and other styles, like the bolero (pronounced *boh-LEH-roh*) and guajira (pronounced *gwah-HEE-rah*). In most cases, the cha-cha bell is played with the shoulder of the stick on the mouth of the cowbell.

MARACAS

Maracas are a pair of percussion instruments made from gourds, round plastic or leather containers, or any material that will hold beads. These containers are then mounted on handles. Maracas are played by holding one handle in each hand and shaking the instruments.

Typically, one of the maracas is higher pitched than the other. To find the difference in pitch, hold the instrument by the handle and move your wrists up and down. This procedure will allow you to feel the weight of the beads and to hear the difference in pitch. Once you find the higher-pitched maraca, hold it with your right hand and play the notes that fall on the beat. Use the lower-pitched maraca to play the upbeats.

JOSÉ ANTONIO DIAZ

Example C

Maracas

EL CAYUCO

by Tito Puente

Oye cayuco

OH-yeh kah-YOO-koh

Oye mi cha-cha-cha

OH-yeh mee chah-chah-CHAH

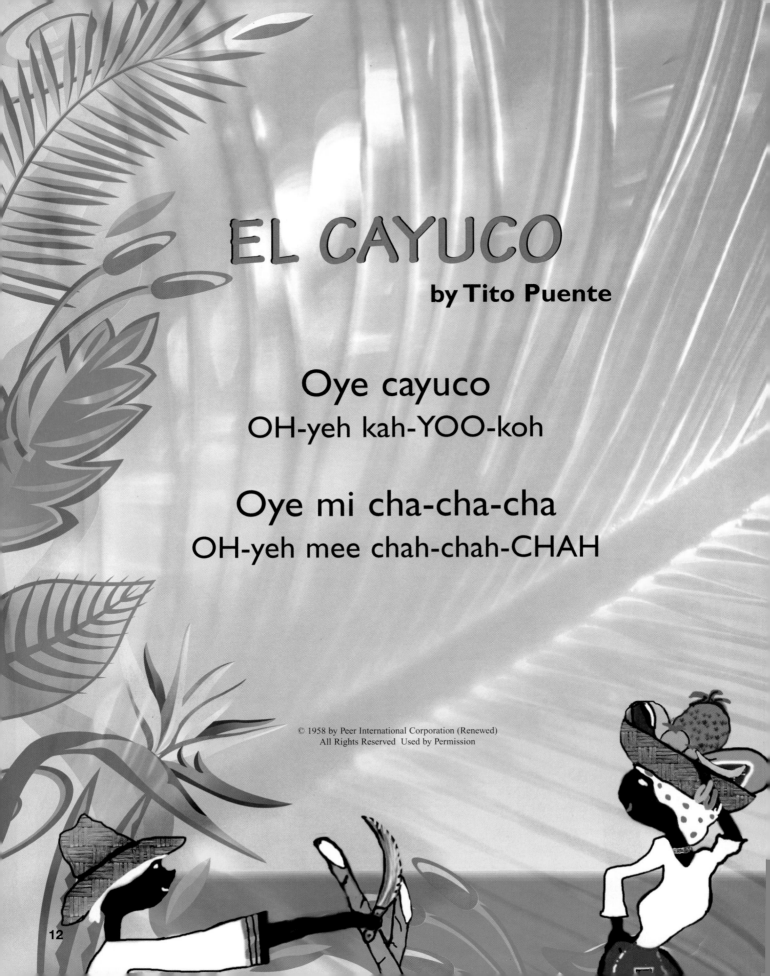

Tito Puente

Tito Puente (1923–2000) was regarded by many as "The King of Latin Music." He was an influential performer, composer, arranger, percussionist, and ambassador for Afro-Cuban music. Puente recorded more than 100 songs and published more than 400 compositions. Puente was honored with many Grammy Awards. He is best known for his hit tune "Oye Cómo Va."

THE
Cha-Cha
RHYTHM

The cha-cha rhythm is the simplest of the Afro-Cuban dance rhythms. It is driven by quarter notes. The cha-cha rhythm can be found in other styles of music. Pop music artists such as Marc Anthony and Jennifer Lopez often use the cha-cha rhythm in their music.

Güiro

The güiro is an important instrument in the performance of the cha-cha rhythm. This instrument adds a scraping sound to the texture. Traditionally made from a gourd, the güiro has wide grooves and is played by scraping up and down across the grooves with a small stick.

JOSÉ ANTONIO DIAZ

Güiro

JOSÉ ANTONIO DIAZ

Conga Drum

One of the most important Afro-Cuban instruments is the conga drum. The conga drum has its origins in West Africa. This instrument was made from tree trunks with calfskin stretched over the top and attached with wooden pegs and/or rope. The most common part performed on the conga drum is a pattern called *tumbao* (pronounced *toom-BOW*).

Tumbao is the basic conga drum pattern used in son-related rhythms. The following is a basic tumbao used in the cha-cha rhythm:

JOSÉ ANTONIO DIAZ

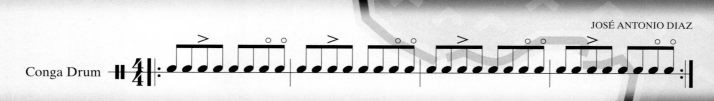

Open Tone

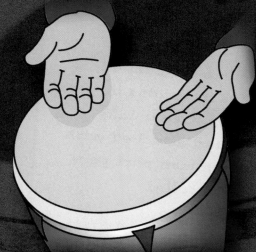

Marcha
(MAHR-shah)

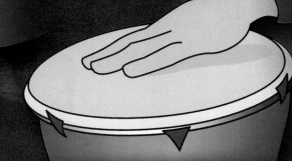

Muted Slap

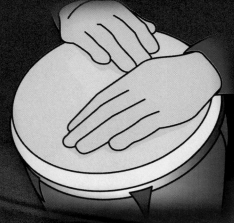

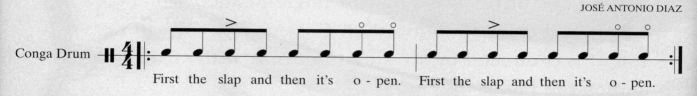

JOSÉ ANTONIO DIAZ

Conga Drum

First the slap and then it's o - pen. First the slap and then it's o - pen.

TIMBALES

The **timbales** are a pair of single-headed, tunable metal drums mounted on a stand. The timbales' sound is produced by striking the drum with sticks and/or the hand.

At first, timbales were used only by Cuban ensembles called charanga orchestras, which made the cha-cha dance style popular. These groups were also interpreters of a song style called **danzón** (pronounced *dahn-SOHN*).

The instrumentation of these groups consisted of strings, woodwinds, güiro, conga, and timpani. The timpani later evolved in the 1940s to what we now know as timbales. Today, the timbales are a major contributor to the Afro-Cuban sound. The standard timbales set-up includes cowbells, woodblocks, a cha-cha bell, and a cymbal.

JOSÉ ANTONIO DIAZ

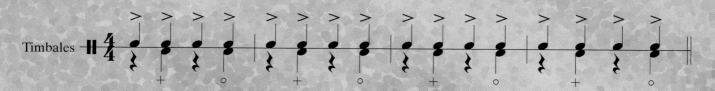

Timbales

Cha-Cha

Dancing

Dancing is a very expressive art form. Different cultures throughout the world use dance as part of a sacred ritual or as a means to celebrate special events.

Afro-Cuban music is also expressed through dance. Many of the Afro-Cuban rhythms are associated with a particular dance. For example, the cha-cha rhythm was named cha-cha because of the scraping sounds dancers' feet make when dancing to this rhythm.

Performers of Afro-Cuban music often dance as they play the music. Dancing allows performers of this music to feel the rhythm and the pulse.

Just a Little Cha-cha

JOSÉ ANTONIO DIAZ

24

Just a Little Cha-Cha - 10 - 9

BOLERO

Bolero is a ballad with a slow tempo and strong rhythmic pulse. The lyrics of these ballads are usually about romance. The development of this genre can be traced back to the Spanish troubadours in the eighteenth century. The troubadours would usually accompany themselves with their guitars. Some scholars believe that the term *bolero* was derived from the guitar-strumming troubadours called *bolerear* (pronounced *boh-leh-reh-AHR*).

The rhythmic element of this style can be found in some of America's popular music.

2-3 Son Clave

JOSÉ ANTONIO DIAZ

CONGA DRUM

Open Tones

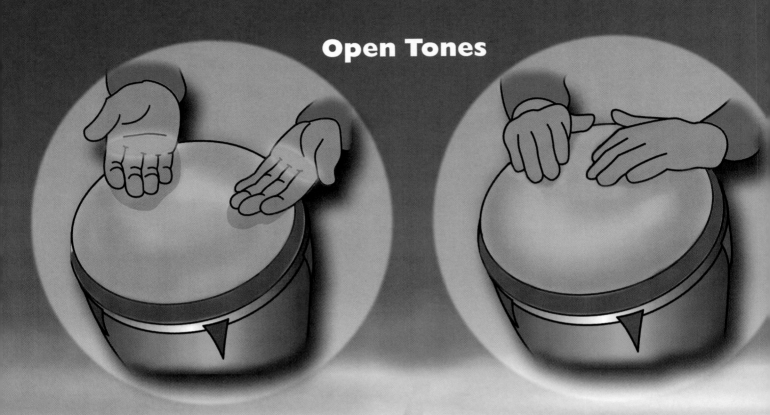

Slap

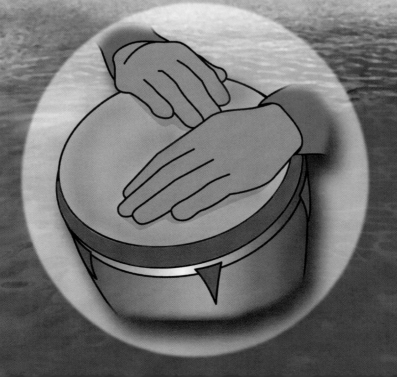

Conga Drum Bolero Rhythm

JOSÉ ANTONIO DIAZ

Learning the
Conga Drum Bolero Rhythm

JOSÉ ANTONIO DIAZ

I move slow be-cause I love you. I move slow be-cause I love you.

Bongos

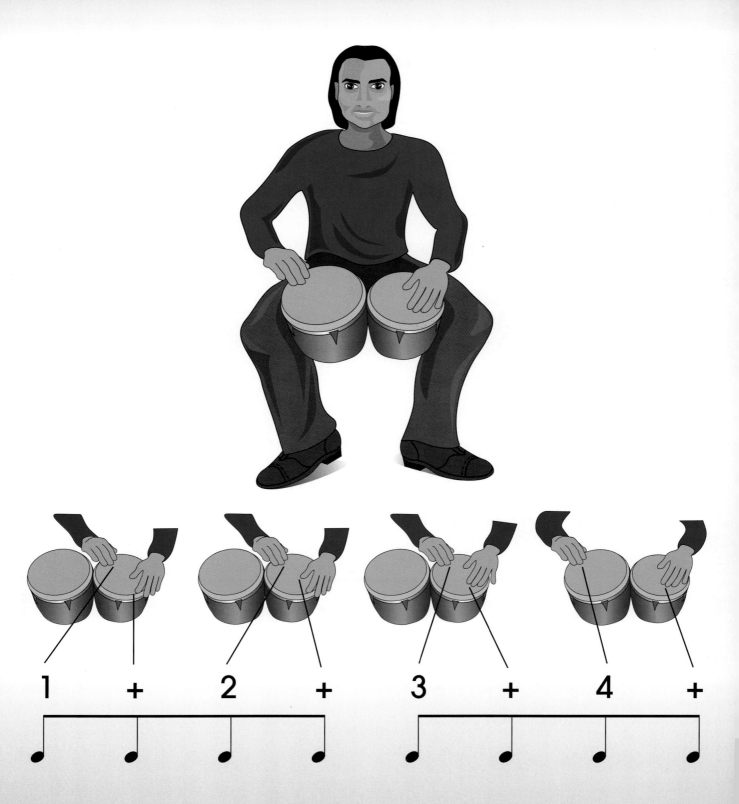

1   +   2   +   3   +   4   +

Bongos

The **bongos** are a pair of high-pitched drums
that can be mounted on a stand. This instrument
can be played while standing or placed between
the knees while sitting. The basic rhythmic
pattern played on the bongos is called **martillo**
(pronounced *mahr-TEE-yoh*), which literally means
"hammer." The bongo part for the bolero is
a one-measure repeated pattern.
This pattern is composed of even eighth notes
throughout the measure.

Bongos Bolero Rhythm

JOSÉ ANTONIO DIAZ

MARACAS

Maracas Bolero Rhythm

JOSÉ ANTONIO DIAZ

TIMBALES

Timbales Bolero Rhythm

JOSÉ ANTONIO DIAZ

Timbales

R L L R L R L R L   R L L R L R L R L   R L L R L R L R L   R L L R L R L R L

Claves

Bongos

Maracas

Conga Drum

42

Timbales

Bolero Layering

JOSÉ ANTONIO DIAZ

Bolero Layering - 5 - 1

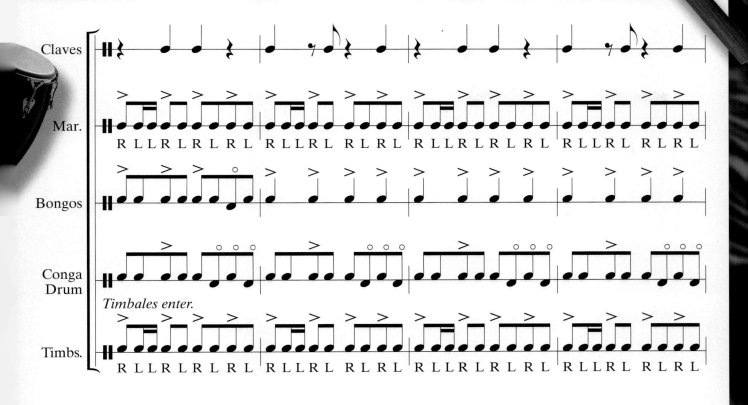

Celia CRUZ

Celia Cruz (1925–2003) is one of the most important females in Afro-Cuban music. Considered by many as "The Queen of Salsa" or "La Guarachera de Cuba" (pronounced *lah gwah-rah-CHEH-rah deh KOO-bah*), Celia Cruz performed for more than 50 years. She released more than 70 albums and appeared in ten movies. Cruz received many of the music industry's highest accolades, including five Grammy Awards and two Latin Grammy Awards.

Guantanamera

Refrain:
Guantanamera, Guajira Guantanamera.
Guantanamera, Guajira Guantanamera.

Yo soy un hombre sincero,
De donde crece la palma,
Y antes de morirme quiero,
Echar mis versos del alma.

Mi verso es de un verde claro,
Y de un carmín encendido,
Mi verso es un ciervo herido,
Que busca en el monte amparo.

Con los pobres de la tierra,
Quiero yo mi suerte echar,
El arroyo de la sierra,
Me complace más que el mar.

Note: Repeat refrain after each of the above verses.

English translation
Guantanamera, Guajira Guantanamera.
Guantanamera, Guajira Guantanamera.

I am a sincere man
From a place where the palm grows,
And before I die, I want
To say the verses from my soul.

My verse is light green
And bright red,
My verse is a wounded red deer
That seeks shelter in the mountains.

With the poor of the earth
I want to share my destiny,
The stream of the mountain range
Pleases me more than the sea.

Pronunciation:

GWAN-tah-nah-MEH-rah,* gwah-HEE-rah
GWAN-tah-nah-MEH-rah
GWAN-tah-nah-MEH-rah, gwah-HEE-rah
GWAN-tah-nah-MEH-rah

mee VEHR-soh ehs deh oon VEHR-deh KLAH-roh
ee deh oon kahr-MEEN ehn-sehn-DEE-doh
mee VEHR-soh ehs oon see-EHR-voh eh-REE-doh
keh BOOS-kah ehn ehl MOHN-teh ahm-PAH-roh.

joh soy oon OHM-breh seen-SEH-roh*
deh DOHN-deh KREH-seh lah PAHL-ma
ee AHN-tehs deh moh-REER-meh kee-EH-roh
eh-CHAHR mees VEHR-sohs dehl AHL-mah

kohn lohs POH-brehs deh lah tee-EH-rrah**
kee-EH-roh joh mee soo-EHR-teh eh-CHAHR
ehl ah-RROH-joh deh lah see-EH-rrah
meh kohm-PLAH-seh mahs keh ehl mahr

* *r* in *rah* and *roh* is pronounced with a single flip of the tongue, like the American English pronunciation of *tt* in *bottle*.
** *rr* is strongly trilled.

During the cha-cha, the piano and guitar play **block chords** in rhythm. Block chords are chords in which all notes in the chord sound at the same time.

Block Chords

JOSÉ ANTONIO DIAZ

Piano

The guajira rhythm calls for **broken chords.** In broken chords, the notes sound one at a time. Broken chords are also called **arpeggios.** This pattern is usually played on piano or guitar.

Broken Chords

JOSÉ ANTONIO DIAZ

Piano

GUAJIRA

Guajira (pronounced *gwah-HEE-rah*) is a song style originating with the Cuban peasants and containing elements of the Spanish canción and the Cuban son dance form. Similar to the American blues form, the lyrics of the guajira song style are usually sad or nostalgic. The typical instrumentation of the percussion section in guajira is bongos, congas, timbales, cowbells, maracas, and güiro.

Guajira

Cha-Cha Bell

JOSÉ ANTONIO DIAZ

Cha-cha Bell

Maracas

JOSÉ ANTONIO DIAZ

Maracas

Güiro

JOSÉ ANTONIO DIAZ

Güiro

Conga Drum

JOSÉ ANTONIO DIAZ

Conga Drum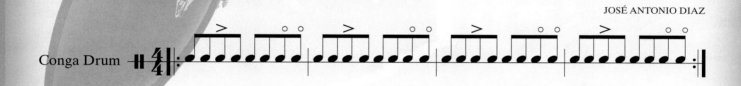

Timbales

JOSÉ ANTONIO DIAZ

Timbales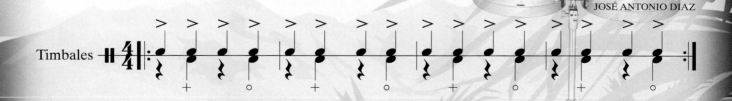

CUBA

- Havana
- Matanzas
- Pinar del Río
- Santa Clara
- Cienfuegos
- Sancti Spíritus
- Ciego de Ávila
- Camagüey
- Las Tunas
- Province of Oriente
- Santiago de Cuba
- Guantánamo

Son Montuno

Son montuno (pronounced *sohn mohn-TOO-noh*) is a popular Cuban dance form. This musical form originated in the province of Oriente (pronounced *oh-ree-EHN-teh*), a mountain region of Cuba. Son montuno means "songs of the mountains" and was performed mainly by peasant farmers. The term **son** comes from the Spanish word *sonetas* (pronounced *soh-NEH-tahs*). Sonetas are poems set to music. The word montuno comes from the word montaña (pronounced *mohn-TAH-nyah*), which means "mountains." Originally, a tres (guitar) and claves were the typical instrumentation of the son montuno. Dance bands first adapted the son montuno rhythm in the 1920s. These groups added the bongos, bass, and trumpet to the ensemble. Typically, the montuno section of the son montuno features vocal and instrumental improvisations.

CHA-CHA

4/4 Four Beats per Measure

JOSÉ ANTONIO DIAZ

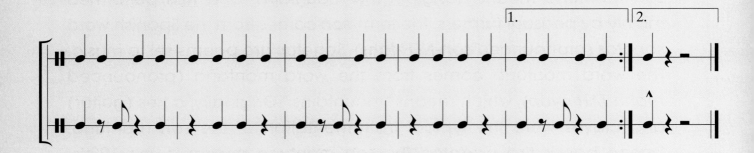

CONGA DRUM
TUMBAO PATTERN

JOSÉ ANTONIO DIAZ

Play four times.

SON MONTUNO

₵ Two Beats per Measure

JOSÉ ANTONIO DIAZ

Foot Tap

Claves

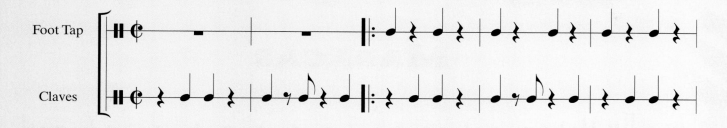

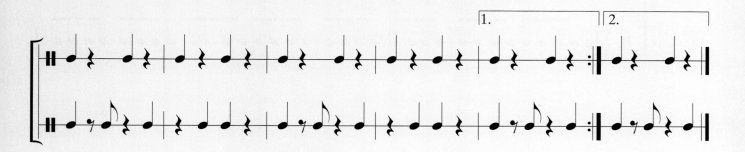

BONGOS
(MARTILLO)

JOSÉ ANTONIO DIAZ

Play four times.

Claves

Bongos

SON MONTUNO

MARACAS

JOSÉ ANTONIO DIAZ

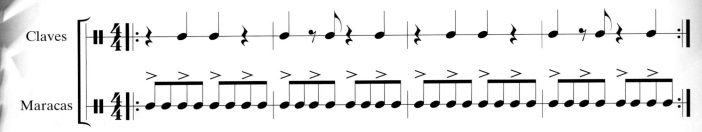

GÜIRO

JOSÉ ANTONIO DIAZ

CÁSCARA

The rhythm pattern played on the shell of the high drum is called **cáscara** (pronounced *KAHS-kah-rah*). Cáscara literally means "shell."

TIMBALES
LEARNING THE CÁSCARA

JOSÉ ANTONIO DIAZ

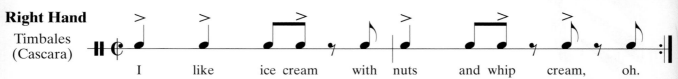

I like ice cream with nuts and whip cream, oh.

TIMBALES
(CÁSCARA)

JOSÉ ANTONIO DIAZ

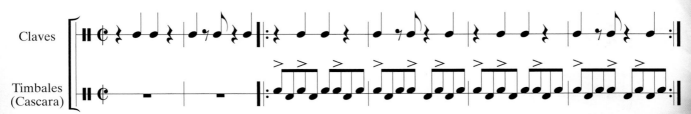

Right Hand and Left Hand: R L R L R R L R R L R R L R L R R L R L R R L R R L R R L R L R

Son Montuno Layering

JOSÉ ANTONIO DIAZ

Claves begin.

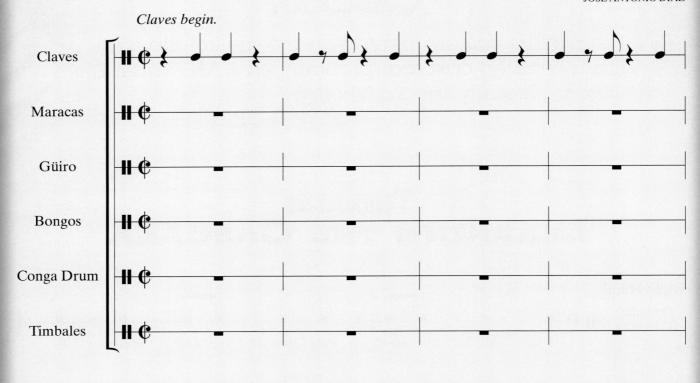

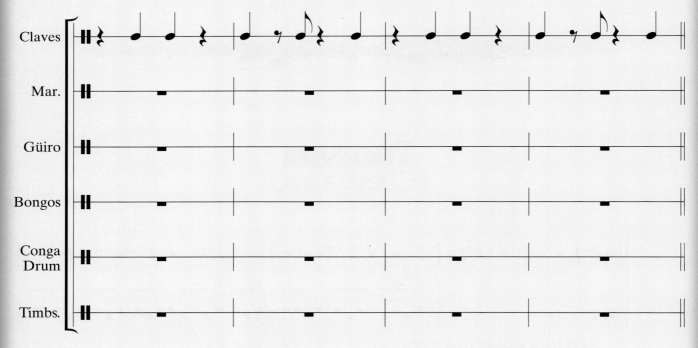

Son Montuno Layering - 6 - 1

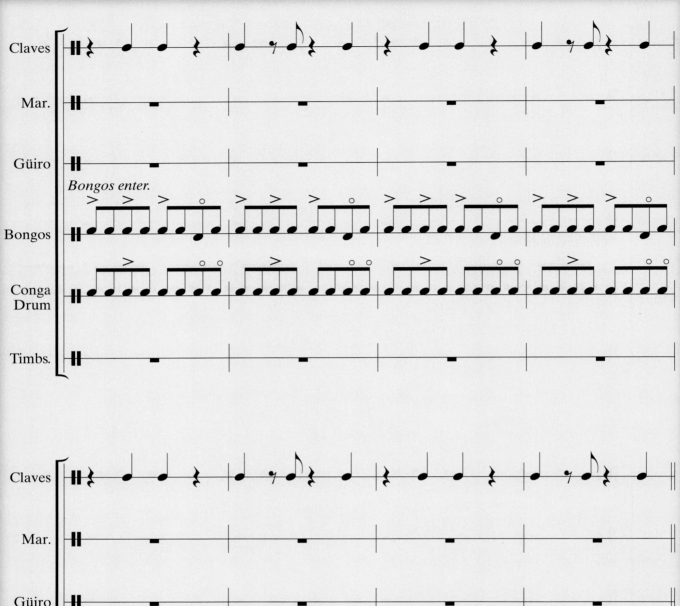

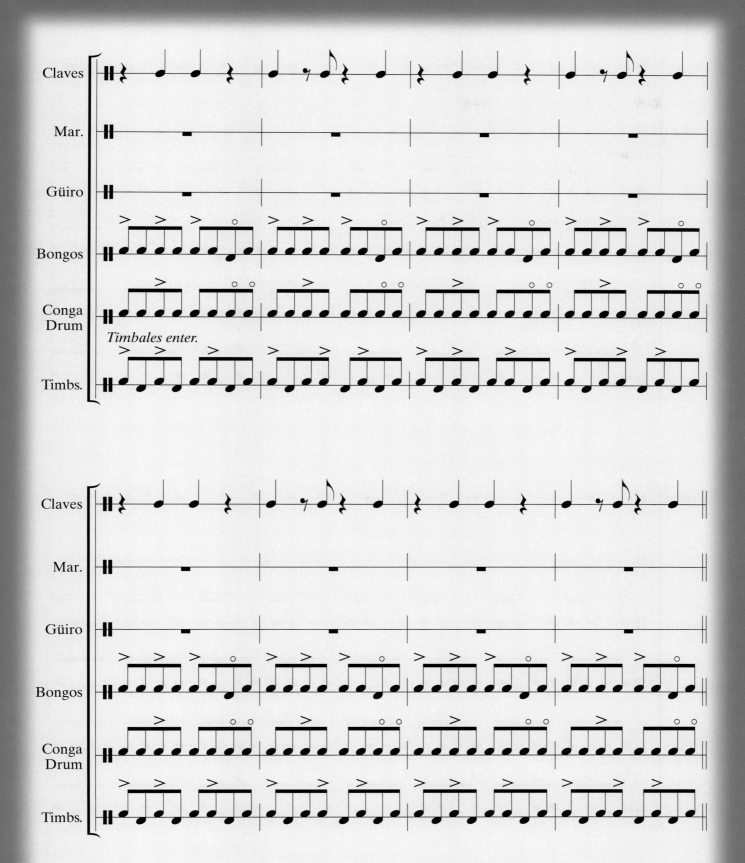

Son Montuno Layering - 6 - 4

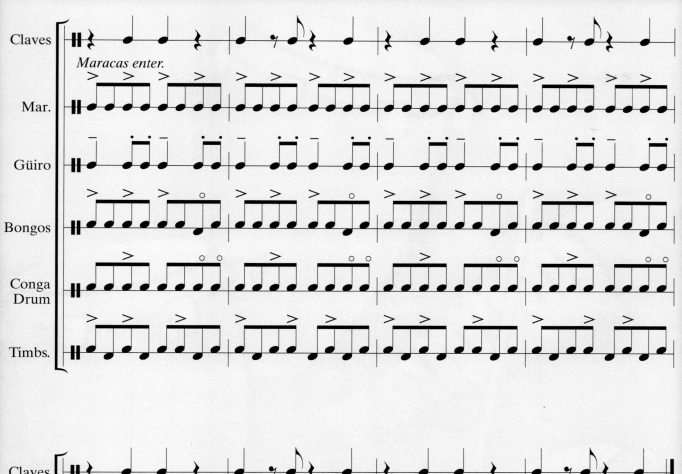

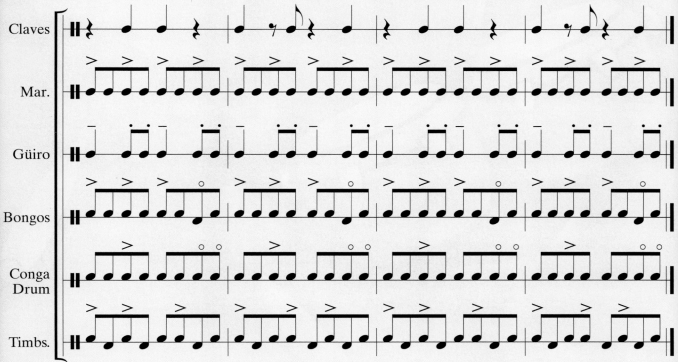

Son Montuno Layering - 6 - 6

Vamos a Gozar

JOSÉ ANTONIO DIAZ

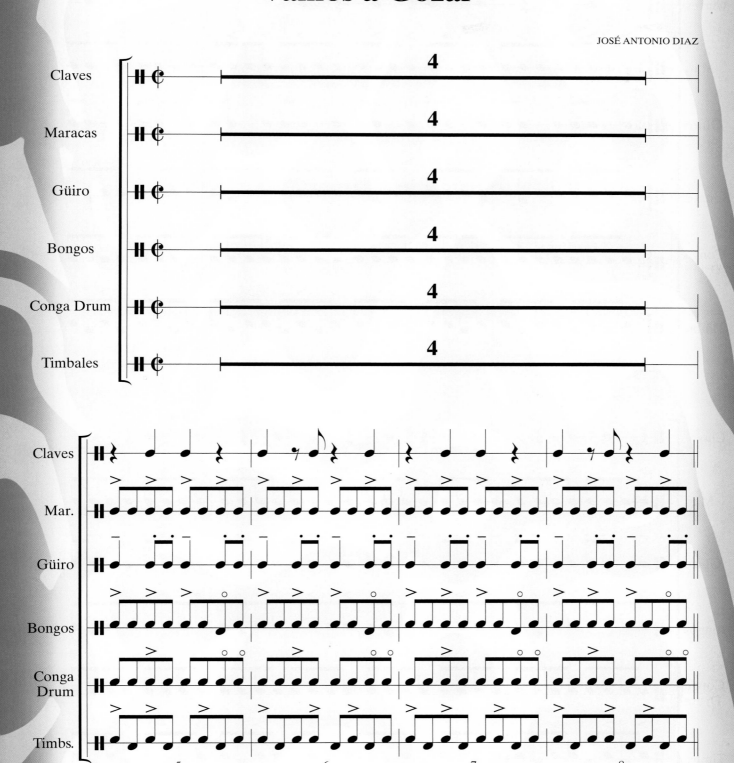

Vamos a Gozar - 3 - 1

67

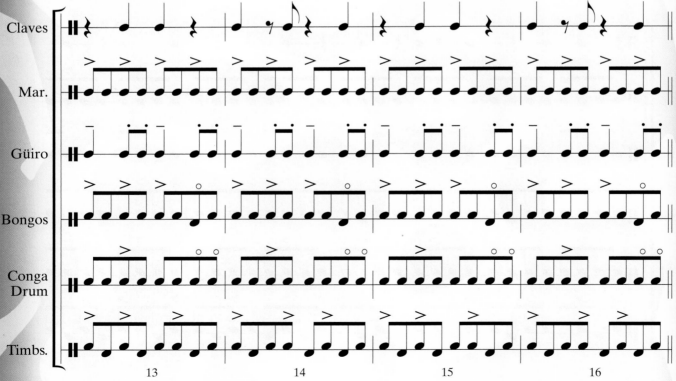

Cha-Cha Rhythm

JOSÉ ANTONIO DIAZ

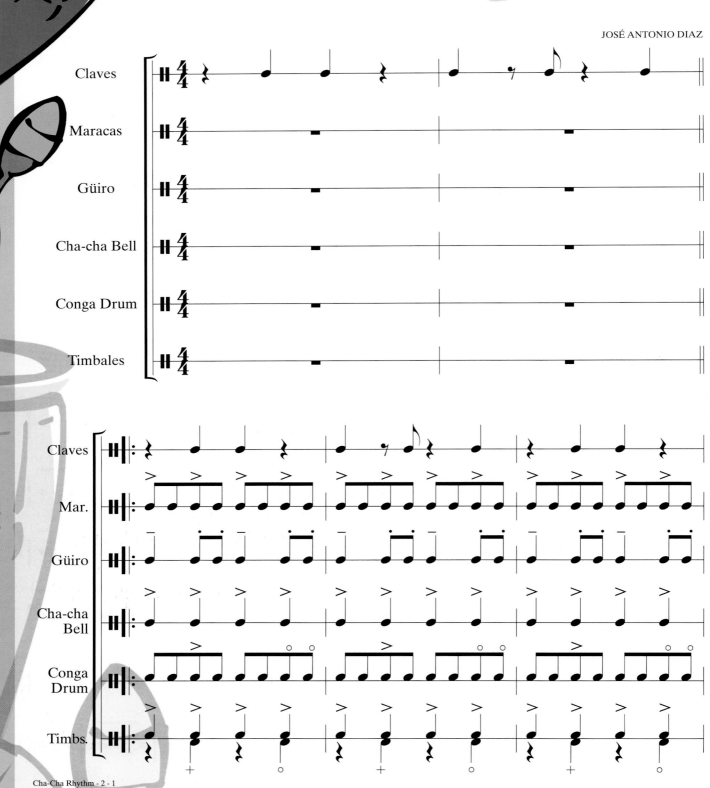

Cha-Cha Rhythm - 2 - 1

70

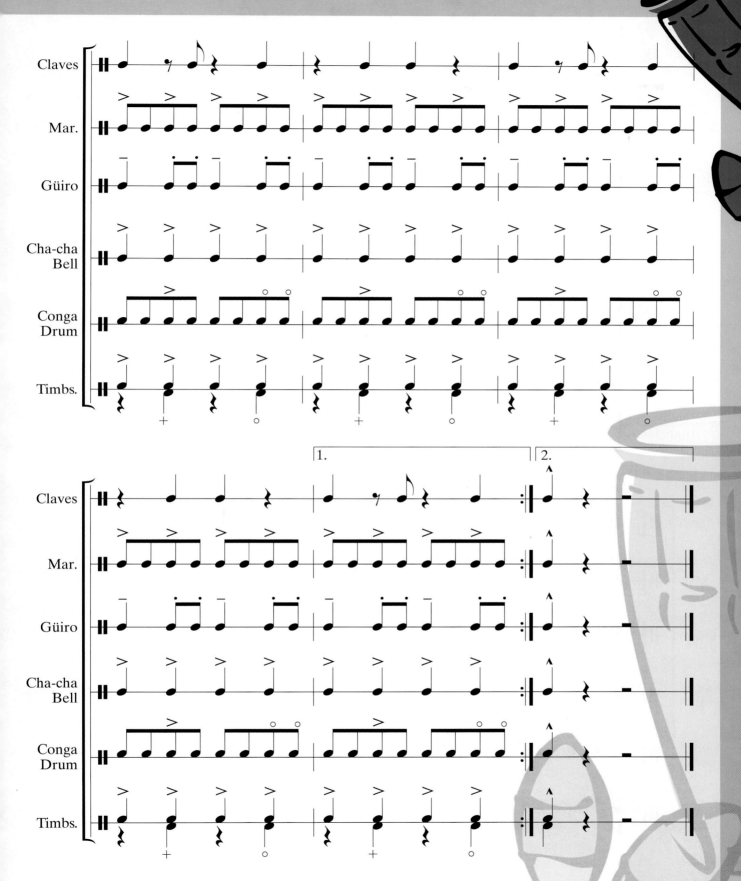

Guajíra Rhythm

JOSÉ ANTONIO DIAZ

Play 5 times.

Son Montuno Rhythm

JOSÉ ANTONIO DIAZ

Son Montuno Rhythm - 2 - 1

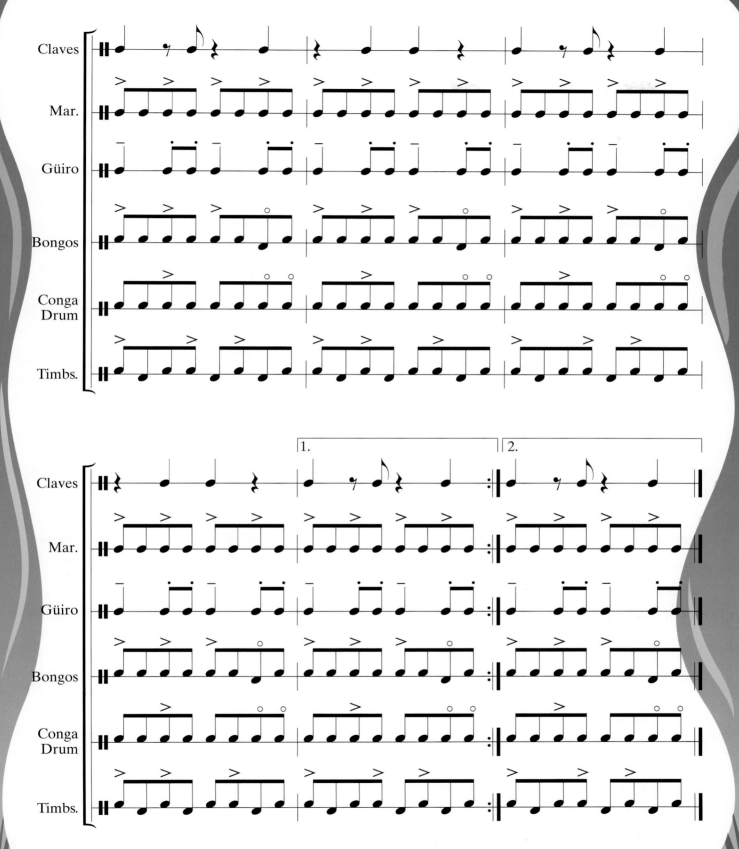

Son Montuno Rhythm - 2 - 2

Glossary

TERMS

3-2 son clave pattern (forward clave)	A rhythm pattern in which the accents fall on beat 1, the "and" of beat 2, and beat 4 of measure 1, and on beats 2 and 3 of measure 2 (page 4)
2-3 son clave pattern (reverse clave)	A rhythm pattern in which the accents fall on beats 2 and 3 of measure 1, and on beat 1, the "and" of beat 2, and beat 4 of measure 2; the measures are played in reverse order from the 3-2 son clave pattern (page 5)
block chords	Chords in which all notes sound at the same time (page 50)
bolero	A Spanish ballad with a slow tempo and strong rhythmic pulse (page 34)
broken chords (arpeggios)	Chords in which the notes sound one at a time (page 51)
call-and-response	A simple musical idea that is played or sung (call) and then responded to with a similar musical idea (response)
cáscara	The rhythm pattern played on the shells (sides) of the timbales; also refers to the shells themselves (page 59)
cha-cha	A Cuban dance rhythm and musical style (pages 6, 14)
clave	A five-note, two-measure rhythm pattern that serves as the fundamental rhythmic pattern for Afro-Cuban music
conga drum	A large, hollow, single-headed West African drum played with the hands (page 17)
forward clave	Another name for the 3-2 son clave pattern
guajira	A song style similar to the cha-cha, with a Cuban origin and Spanish influence
heel-fingers motion	A method of striking the conga drum that involves rocking between the heel of the hand and the fingertips, and yields a muffled tone (page 18)
layering	The process of introducing one musical part at a time to establish a groove
marcha/march	Other names for heel-fingers motion (page 18)
martillo	The basic bongo rhythm pattern; its name means "hammer" (page 39)
muted slap	A drum sound produced by resting the left hand on the drum to stop the vibration while striking the conga toward the edge of the drum with the right hand, which is slightly cupped (page 18)
open tone	The natural open sound of the drum, produced by hitting the drum with the area of the hand that is just below the fingers toward the palm (page 18)
reverse clave	Another name for the 2-3 son clave pattern
son	From the Spanish word *sonetas* (pronounced *soh-NEH-tahs*), which are poems set to music (page 55)
son clave	The most common clave pattern
son montuno	A popular son dance form originating in the province of Oriente, a mountain region of Cuba (pages 54–55)
tumbao	The basic conga drum rhythm pattern (page 17)

INSTRUMENTS

bongos	A pair of high-pitched drums that can be played either held between the knees while sitting or mounted on a stand (pages 38–39)
cha-cha bell	A small, high-pitched bell that is used extensively in the cha-cha and played by striking the shoulder of the stick on the mouth of the bell (page 9)
claves	Two wooden sticks that, when struck together, produce a high-pitched sound (page 8)
conga drum	Originally made from tree trunks with calfskin stretched over the top and attached with wooden pegs and/or rope, played with the hands while sitting with the drum positioned between the knees (page 17)
güiro	Traditionally made from a gourd, this instrument has wide grooves and is played by scraping up and down across the grooves with a small stick (page 15)
maracas	A pair of percussion instruments made from gourds or round plastic or leather containers filled with beads, mounted on handles, and played by shaking (pages 10–11)
timbales	A pair of single-headed, tunable metal drums mounted on a stand and played by striking with sticks and using the hands for muting or other effects (page 20)

Glossary *continued*

MUSICAL SYMBOLS

accent—*A symbol indicating that the note should receive more emphasis than the surrounding notes*

bar line—*A line that goes from the bottom to the top of a staff and divides the staff into measures*

bass clef—*The clef for lower vocal and instrumental parts*

breath mark—*Used to indicate where a singer or wind instrument player should breathe*

clef—*A symbol placed at the beginning of a staff to identify the lines and spaces*

coda—*A short ending section of music*

common time—*The symbol for 4/4 time, or common time*

crescendo—*Gradually becoming louder*

dal segno (D.S.)—*Go back to the ℅ sign and resume singing or playing from there*

D.S. ℅ al Coda **dal segno al coda**— *Go back to the ℅ sign and resume singing or playing from there, until you see "To Coda ⊕"; then go to the Coda section and continue until the end*

decrescendo—*Gradually becoming softer*

double bar line—*Two bar lines placed at the end of a staff to point out the end of a section or composition*

fermata—*A symbol that means to hold or pause (all parts), or stretch the sound longer than it normally would be heard or performed*

flat—*A symbol that lowers the pitch of a note one half step*

f **forte**—*A mark in music that tells musicians to perform at a loud or strong dynamic level*

grand staff—*A set of staves joined together that indicates the joined staves should be performed as one staff*

line note—*A written note with a staff line through its center*

mf **mezzo forte**—*Medium loud*

mp **mezzo piano**—*Medium soft*

natural—*Neither sharp nor flat; a symbol that cancels an existing sharp or flat, changing the tone by one half step*

pp **pianissimo**—*Very soft*

p **piano**—*A mark in music that tells musicians to perform at a soft or quiet dynamic level*

repeat sign—*Two dots in the second and third spaces in front of a double bar line telling you to play or sing the section of music over again from the beginning. A forward repeat sign has two dots after*

the double bar line and tells you to repeat only from that point on.

sharp—*A symbol that raises the pitch of a note one half step*

slur—*A curved line connecting different notes on a staff to indicate they are to be performed smoothly*

space note—*A note written between the lines on a staff*

staccato—*A symbol that indicates the note should be short, or detached from the surrounding notes*

staff—*Five lines and four spaces on which notes and other musical symbols are placed*

staves—*More than one staff*

tie—*A curved line connecting or tying together two notes of the same pitch indicating they are to be played as if they were one note*

3/4, 4/4 time signature—*The symbol at the beginning of the staff that indicates the meter. The upper number indicates the number of beats in each measure, and the lower number indicates which kind of note receives the beat.*

treble clef—*The clef for higher vocal and instrumental parts*

NOTES AND RESTS

♬♬ sixteenth notes

♫ eighth notes

♪♩. eighth quarter dot (eighth dotted quarter)

♩ quarter note

♩. quarter note dot (dotted quarter)

♩. ♪ quarter dot eighth (dotted quarter eighth)

𝄽 quarter rest

𝅗𝅥 half note

𝅗𝅥. half note dot (dotted half)

▬ half rest

𝅝 whole note

▬ whole rest

♪♩♪ syncopa (eighth quarter eighth)

Index

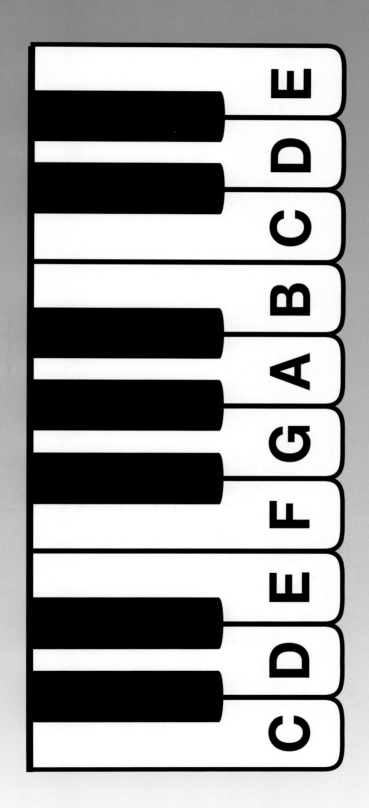

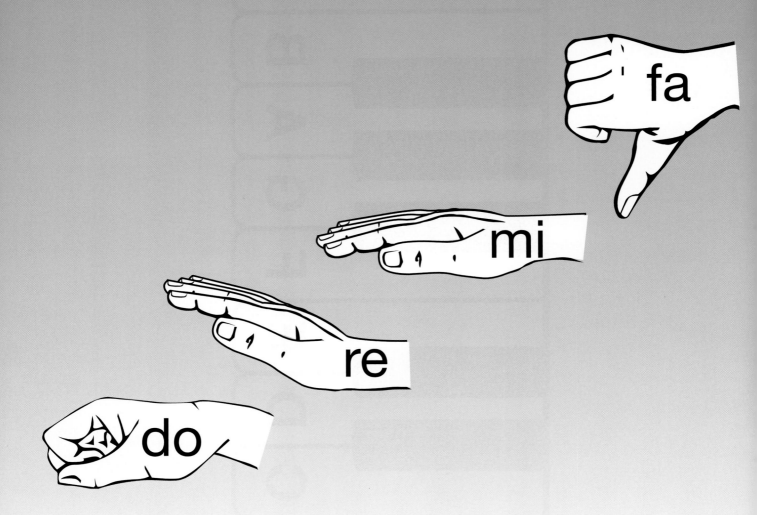

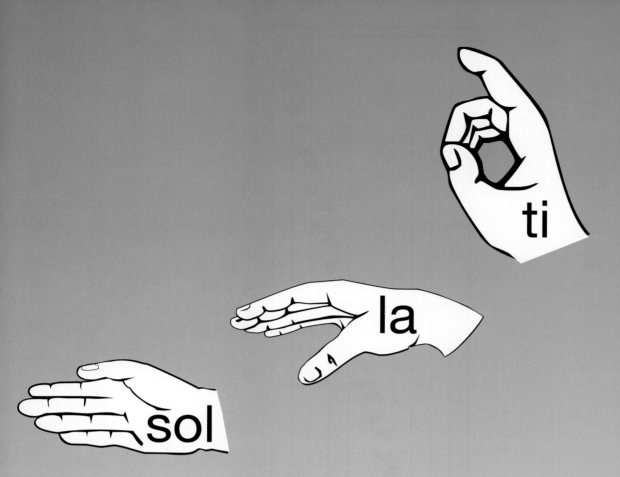

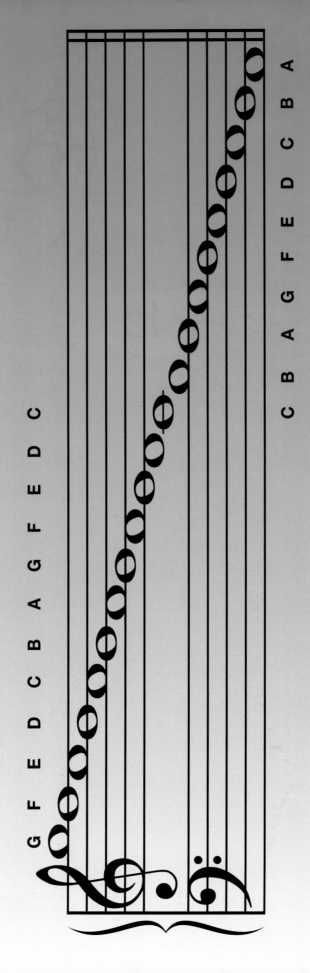